I0764642

The World That Isn't There

THE WORLD THAT ISN'T THERE

Poems by

Wil Mills

Edited by

Kathryn Oliver Mills

Measure Press
Evansville, Indiana

Printed in the United States of America
First Edition

The text of this book is composed in Baskerville.
Edited by Kathryn Oliver Mills
Composition by R.G.
Manufacturing by Ingram.

Mills, Wil, 1969–2011
The World That Isn't There / by Wil Mills — 1st ed.

ISBN-13: 978-1-939574-22-0
ISBN-10: 1-939574-22-6
Library of Congress Control Number: 2017910267

Measure Press
526 S. Lincoln Park Dr.
Evansville, IN 47714
http://www.measurepress.com/measure/

Acknowledgments

Because Wil had not yet begun to shape these poems into a manuscript, I want to express my particular gratitude to Tim Steele, Alan Shapiro, and Raymond Oliver for commenting on this manuscript as I was editing it. Many thanks also to the poets who wrote such thoughtful blurbs for this book, to Benjamin for illustrating his father's work, and to Rob Griffith for his generous help throughout the publishing process.

— Kathryn Oliver Mills

For Benjamin and Phoebe-Agnès, and for all those to whom these poems speak.

CONTENTS

I.

Diluvian Dream 1
Gas Ghazal 2
Monteagle Farmer 4
Last Laugh 6
For the Unemployed Man at Forty 7
Sans-abri 9
Urban Vignette I 10
Uncle Sam's Angina 11
Baby Dolls 12
A Young Priest's Wife Begins to Think 13
Urban Vignette II 16
Pop's Happy Land and Truck Stop 17
Genius Loci 19

II.

Diluvian Delusion 23
Relative 24
Facebook 2 25
Tangere 26
Praying Hands 27
Contingo 28
Imitatio Humana 29
Crosswalk 30
April 28 31
Global Eyes 32
Nominal Problem 33
Looking Up through the Cracks 34
Intellectual Lust 35

Word-of-Mouth 36
Rebuilding Babel 37
Reductio Ad Absurdam 38
Credo Quia Absurdam Est 39
Eden *Redux* as Apocalypse 40

III.

Double Vision 43
Apocalyptic Almanac 44
Fallen Fruit 45
Littoral Translation 47
Imago Reperta 48
Dream Vocation 49
The Culture Counter of the Counter Culture 50
Guru 51
OMG 52
Irreconcilable 53
Modern Church Architecture 54
Chapel of the Cross 55
Bruegel's Harvesters 56
Nude Descending an Escalator 60
Nashville Wasteland 61
Hope 73
Spiro/Spirare 74
Snowman Argument 75
Satanic Christmas 77
Out on My Word 78
Seriously Funny 79
Telos 81
Ruach 82
Questions in a Doctor's Waiting Room 83

I.

Diluvian Dream

All afternoon I walk behind the mower,
Imagining, though paradoxically,
That even though the grass is getting lower,
What I have cut is like a rising sea;
The parts I haven't cut, with every pass,
Resemble real geography, a map,
A shrinking island continent of grass
Where shoreline vanishes with every lap.

At last, the noise and smell of gasoline
Dispel my dream. What sea? Peninsulas?
They were the lands my inner child had seen,
Their little Yucatans and Floridas.

But when I'm finished, and Yard goes back to Lawn,
I can't help thinking that a world is gone.

Gas Ghazal

He used to love the smell of gasoline
When his father went to Shell for gasoline,

And fumes at the pump made corrugated ripples,
Pleating the air and nozzle of gasoline.

When filling mower tanks, he loved the point
When funnels overflowed, spilling gasoline.

Two-cycle chainsaw engines burning oil,
Mixing the air so well with gasoline;

Fuel leaking around his Evenrude
In prism-clouds of lovely gasoline . . .

Those were the days when every gas cap held
A promise, a whiff, the thrill of gasoline.

But Briggs & Stratton led to Motocross
And dirt-bike circles. Miles for gasoline.

Then truck and tractor pulls, and NASCAR races.
It was all a race, pell-mell for gasoline.

And even later, when the heady joy was over,
He bought a Yukon that swilled his gasoline.

The sun felt brighter through the moonroof glare,
UV and SUV, both ills of gasoline,

Both gone unnoticed, like the residue
Of lead around him, (tell-tale gasoline)

Like the pterodactyl in a plastic bag,
Crude dinosaurs from wells of gasoline,

Like Teflon particles inside his heart,
Flooding him up to the gills in gasoline.

"O, carburetor-turbocharger-love!"
He knew, then, that he'd kill for gasoline.

"Floor me, Baby!" But the love was gone,
Pedal to the metal with a lot of gasoline.

His helicopter flew across the sun
With airplane vapor trails of gasoline.

How beautiful! But, oh, the arcing wire,
The fire, the melted line of gasoline.

It always was his dream to burn, to char,
His flesh combustible as gasoline,

And leave the world the way the world began,
Leaving nothing but the smell of gasoline

In roadside crosses made of PVC,
The testament and will of gasoline.

Monteagle Farmer

An angus herd and one white cross-breed cow
Fill up the shadow of a single oak,
And, since it hasn't rained in over a month,
They almost disappear in heat and steam
That wavers upward from their salty hides.

The farmer passes them without a glance.
He walks so slow that you can see his pace
Conforming to the speed of cattle breath,
The speed of clouds. If he moved any slower
There wouldn't be a verb to him; he'd be
A noun, is all. And yet he's both, a place
That places him.
                                        He walks along a trail
That cows have cut by winding single file.
He's going fishing, cane pole, cork, and worms,
The way he did when he was just a boy
And never quit.
                                        It seems like every day
Somebody dies who used to fish that way,
By poling, wasting daylight's precious hours;
Occupation for the penny-foolish;
Pound-wise pastime for the profligate.

The worlds of people he will never know
Keep racing past on highway 41.
Across the road they go about their business,
Moving faster than the clouds it seems,

Fast food, hotels, a grocery store, all lifting
Names for what they are on metal poles.

The farmer wouldn't sell and wouldn't sell,
So now his barn has been surrounded by
The pseudo-city of the interstate.
From there you notice how his window trim
Is painted orange for the football team.
His wife smokes cigarettes to beat the band.

At dusk his shadow thins and blinks below
The scraggly sycamores between his house
And tractor shed.
                                        He's caught a mess of fish.
The county health official told him once
He shouldn't eat them since his ponds are tainted:
Seepage from the septic fields, and mercury.
He eats them anyhow. He doesn't care.
Indifference is how he hates the world.

Don't ask him what he thinks about the stores
And filling stations all around his land.
He wouldn't answer. He would stare at you
And blink his eyes so all you'd see is how
The glint of evening sky combines with those
Florescent bulbs that start to buzz and click.

A truck gears down to make the long descent
To Nashville. Angus shadows trail away
To water just beyond the view of cars.
The farmer turns and takes his fish inside
Where he will hate you with a perfect hate.

Last Laugh

More gulls exist at inland parking lots
Than at the sea today. At first, the news
Depressed me. Think of the oceans that have lost
A water bird that even Homer knew.

But watch the laughing gulls that clip and dive
Above a dumpster next to Captain D's;
It's clear that urban sprawl and how we live,
To them, is something gained, not their demise.

Will they devolve the webbing of their claws
To grasp a scrap of ham that can't swim free?
Will they forget the flight that drew them close
To elements Empedocles believed?

I doubt it. I'm the one who's "lost the farm"
(Earth, water, air, and fire), who feels infirm.

For the Unemployed Man at Forty

Prophecy is not about
The future; it isn't fortune telling.
It's more the ache of déjà-vu
Expanded as an open window
That lets you see the obvious
In the free fall, the hydroplane
Of time or mind.
                    It lets you see
The moment when awareness snags
For half a second or less and holds
In *sostenuto* mode, the stream
Around you hurtling on in a blur.
Prophecy tells it like it IS.

And this is a prophecy for you
When backyard deer that used to run
From your scent will almost let you touch them;
When women in the produce section
Hand you the bag but will not smile;
When you clean the garage again and rev
The drill to your head without a bit.

Watch how bacon shrinks in the skillet.
Notice that stainless steel will stain,
That chimneys lean away from eaves.
Study how nursing mothers stare

Into space as if at something, as if
The two imaginary points
That hold perspective all in place
Are gathering and focusing
Their spiderings, their lines of their world.
Forget how you're "reduced to this,"
To understanding how women feel.

Predict the present. Smell the garage,
How tools and old unpainted wood
Remind you of the fishing camp
That's sold, of the old men there, long dead,
Their eyes that burned with gem-like flames,
The eyes of Teddy Roosevelt.
They told you, "Leave no stone unturned,
No urn unstoned." They laughed and spit.
Remember them, and, while you stare
At nothing, think of everything.

Sans-abri

Lying near the whole-grain grocery store
Where open-minded shoppers gourmandize,
He makes a human smudge outside the door.
He doesn't move, and I avert my eyes.

Urban Vignette I

A student in the graduate life of books,
Well over thirty, yet stuck all the same in his teens,
Maintains a pony tail and leather looks
To watch for women wearing denim jeans.
Like rock musicians, he will not age well,
Loving a zipper's guttural descent,
Expensive dope, the two in parallel.
He's both pathetic and magnificent.

Uncle Sam's Angina

Awakened by his radio alarm,
He rises from a dream and sleeping pills
And feels a pain that courses down his arm.
Those leggy women wearing espadrilles
Who giggled as they walked across his back,
Were they a dream?
                                        Oh shit! The bitches stole
My TV. Damn it!
                They did not, in fact;
He turns it on with his remote control.
Montage accelerates inside the box.
Commercials flicker calendars of speed.
The tele-visionaries beat their clocks,
Impatient in the almanacs of greed.
The morning news. The local weather spot.
The anchor-woman shows her tongue a lot.

Baby Dolls

The news today: a whole busload of nuns,
Each raped and murdered on a jungle road.
Who were the men? Who gave them loaded guns?

Across from me, a woman bent and showed
Her bosoms to the world, and I became
The murderers, those hungry birds of prey.

My chromosomes arrange the deadly game.
My genes remember why some people say
The cognate sounds for "vulva:" (*put* or *pute*)

In countries far apart around the globe.
God help each daughter in her birthday suit,
In the lingerie of little girls that strobe

In whirling movements they, too soon, perfect
As dolls made anatomically correct.

A Young Priest's Wife Begins to Think

That day the neighbor's daughter killed herself,
The dogs were barking up and down the street. —
She would've started college in the fall —
Dogs always know, and then, I swear to God,
A painted bunting hit my glass and died.
It's not the neighbor's girl I can't forget
But how that bird was prettier dead than living.
Until you hold one up and spread it out,
You can't make out the colors in their wings.

It rained the day before they found her body,
Angela, or Julie, I don't know.
The children in the neighborhood had scrawled
Their names in mud that slicked along the road.
Their footprints overlapped in cross-out marks.
That night I dreamed that I remembered forward,
Not to know the future, but to be
Where I could then remember back and see
The things I can't make out before my eyes.
I wonder, half of me, if this is bad,
If I've been stealing paper from myself.
But all I got were smells, like sour milk
And starchy patches on the ironing board.
There must be things I'm not supposed to know.

I'm not allowed to dream a reason why
The man who married me had ever thought
I'd be his second chance at love, my God,
When "love" to him means "sex" and little else.
I woke up in a sweat and flopped my arm
Where Daniel should have been. He wasn't there.
Outside, the heavy dew on everything
Was sparkling where the motion lights were lit.
I heard him gasping in the garden shed
And smelled the Vaseline Intensive Care,
And he was saying, "No, I'm not disgusting,"
Over and over, sobbing like a girl.
That's what he's like.
                                        You'd think a priest would be
More spiritual, more . . . I don't know, less needy.
        I can't help him with his dirty urges.

        Then I got it, yeah, I really got it
        When the neighbors asked if he would do
The funeral.
Call me psychic, but I knew:
Those meetings in his study, "counseling."
He must have "helped" her with her fears. Yeah, right.
He did the same for me. I see the pattern.
I told him to do the funcral alone,
Without *me* there, I mean. I have my pride
And puked all afternoon while he was gone.
I lay there on the floor just looking up,
Like how I used to do in college when
I'd smoked a lot of pot and then would think
The whole damn universe had stopped expanding,
Collapsing rapidly backwards on itself,
Searching for the place where it began.

I thought about those back-from-death accounts
Of people on the operating table,
Floating up above themselves with "grandma,"
Or walking down a tunnel towards a light.
They see the stillborn brother no one knew
In houses made of antebellum glass.
That's how I was.
                                        My heaven is a place
Where little girls have never been abused
And painted buntings never ever die.

Urban Vignette II

A regular of the corner coffee house,
He occupies his time and favorite booth,
A man who's known the hatred of his spouse,
Perhaps deserving it.
                                        He's faced the truth
And walks to ward away a heart attack.
There's a rubber band around the paperback
He's brought along; he may or may not peruse it.
Coffee; paper; then home to face the music.

Pop's Happy Land and Truck Stop

The ballad of Grundy County isn't sung.
It isn't even written down, not yet,
Unless you're of a mind to see the need
That rises in a woman's heart, a waitress
There at the truck stop on the interstate.
If you could see how such a thoroughfare
Is like a promise, offering the world
A welcome it cannot deliver, you
Would recognize the rhythm of it all,
How strains of it are ringing here and there.

The waitress might believe in history
If she had learned in school that towns like this
Have always grown around a dock, a port,
A trading post, a watering hole where boys
Forever favor the men who fathered them,
The men who stop for gas and food and leave
A part of them that leads to restlessness,
A state of mind that loves the loud machines
Coursing from boundary to boundary.
But such a history is dead to her.
Reality for her is like a story,
One that refuses to accept the past
And has no future, only now, today
Where truckers slap her on the ass and laugh.
When she was young, she saw all fifty states

By riding with a trucker she had met.
A year went by and she was still not free.
She ended up in Tennessee for good
And never notices the bus depot
Across the street where Greyhound passengers
Descend in single file and mill around.
They smoke one cigarette a-piece then leave.
You'd think she never notices because
Of being too distracted by the truckers
Behind the dusty, two-inch window blinds.
But if you watched her eyes and how they land
On certain things and *not* on too much else,
You'd know she chooses not to see the bus.
Is it an instinct or a conscious thing?
Which ever one, you'd know that if your life
Were slinging hash with chicken strips and gravy,
You wouldn't ever look at buses either.
If your husband lived on disability
And meals of homemade methamphetamine,
You'd hear the music on the radio
Come in and out. The Nashville sound would pass
Right through your heart in waves, in megahertz,
Resolving nothing but the seventh chords.

Genius Loci

At Waffle House beside the interstate,
A waitress works her way through school and talks
To the customers about what's on her plate:
Her mother's cancer, her classes, her boss that stalks
Behind her cracking his whip. "Shut up!"
                                        She learns
Their names, not only the locals', and she walks
A mile in everybody's shoes by turns
And leaps that take her places.
                                    "HERE can dance
Inside of There," she says, but it's clear she yearns
For a world that doesn't blur the two, a chance
To know her place and not some modern myth
Where small trombones make paper clips in France,
Blowing bubbles in Babylon where even our kith
Forgets that "compassion" once meant "suffer with."

II.

Diluvian Delusion

Polaris, in his gig as Cynosure,
Must either labor like a God to be
The focal point our planet spins around,
Or it's a dead-head job, a sinecure.
Or, sacred *and* profane, he still doesn't see
Our turning blur of woodlands being towned.
Or is it all projection on my part to blame
His candle hidden in a distant sconce
For how we fan *and* fail to keep the flame
In *festinate-lente* nonchalance?
The melting arctic ice in the constant sea
Will flood towns *and* our belief in constancy.
We fire ourselves yet play at being God,
Forgetting the spell of Matin *and* Aubade.

Relative

After getting fired at Waffle House,
She sat in air-conditioned furniture stores,
Pretending the sofas, chairs, and cabinet doors
Were in a home, or in the lost-and-found
Of household things that used to have a home.

She sat there reading, thinking: "If you divide
The word "nowhere," you get Now Here." She cried,
And her teardrops only fell on words like *That* and *Whom*.
She'd lost her job for making everyone
Feel touched and spoken for.
                                        There'd been a warning:
"Don't get personal like that, at least not now,
Not here!" She'd told her boss in the beating sun
That Nowhere is a world that keeps on warming . . .

Facebook 2

If Zuckerberg had called it Neighborbook,
Would its absurdity have been more clear?
It's easier "to friend" a neighbor than
To love the person living right next door.

Imagine a bumper sticker bragging that
"I have more friends than you."
                                        Imagine a man,
Your uncle, maybe, in the nursing home;
He lives for bath time, or the casual
And inadvertent brush of a hand, or talk
That's close enough to know his name, his scent.

Imagine a high school girl that others friended
As a joke.
                        Imagine the latest way of Having-
Not in front of the Haves and crying, "Somebody,
Touch my hand. Somebody, talk to me."

Tangere

Lament the motion-activated light
And sliding doors that let you in and out
Of grocery stores.
                                        Question the subtle art
And sleight of hand whereby machines insert
Caesuras of air between what used to be
An even pair of Touch & Thing.
                                                        The eye
That scans your credit card is not alive.
The digital hands of time will never shake.
But human hands emit a small amount
Of infra-red, a healing kind of heat.

Devices *are* divisive, and cold, so let
Your fingers *char* the world and feel it lilt,
Rendering music out of subway ells
With carillons of elevator bells.

Praying Hands

Workmen reach and prune the trees,
Old sycamores cut back in knotted
Postures, clasping knuckleless
As if in awkward prayers of angst.
I saw the same contorted gestures
At the market, Buddha citrons
Shaped like multi-fingered hands.
And near this place on Telegraph
Two nuns on tour from Europe bought
A porcelain hand in bird-position,
Saying, "See, the hand of God!"

It makes me careful how I pray,
Afraid that I have offered thoughts
While unaware of hand or gesture.
Posture doesn't matter, right?
But something lightens in my palm
And climbs when I have prayers to lift,
As now, with workmen reaching up
To prune, these club-fist mutilations
On the sycamores invite a seeking
Motion, what Zacchaeus made,
Hand over hand from limb to life.

Contingo

With a cellphone cricked against her collarbone
And chin, a woman aimed her cheerful gaze
Above the traffic that, beyond her phone
And in her mind, had vanished.
                                                  In a haze,
She gestured with her hand, mid-thought, and stepped
Directly in the path of several cars.
They honked and swerved, avoiding her, except
She didn't notice.
                                    I thanked her lucky stars
For her, my hand involuntarily
Extended in a vain attempt at prayer.

Then, later on the crowded bus, my knee
And elbow pressed on people. I felt my hair
Stand up in unavoidable delight,
In touch, in body language however slight.

Imitatio Humana

In shafts of light I saw where dozens of bugs
Were spiraling a model of DNA,
Perhaps their own. I wasn't taking drugs!

Above me, singing in a tree that day,
A mockingbird did imitations of
The latest cell-phone rings; one hit
B-flat, the key of blues. He did it for love,
But what did it mean?
                                        Hmm . . . I'm winging it . . .
And what if *we* should imitate the bees
That disappear; dead lady bugs in lights;
Or warblers flying south before they freeze,
Mistaking cities for stars on starless nights?

We'd learn the hard way that panes resemble sky,
That even hornets quiver when they die.

Crosswalk

For several days I've watched a robin beat
Herself repeatedly against a window.

An oracle. A bird-sign that augurers
Once understood.
                                        It breaks my heart to see
Her wanting some illusion in the glass
As much as I want things I cannot have:
Assurance that my children never suffer;
An ordinary life where things make sense.

We hurl ourselves at hope. We try to read
The symbolled wonders signaled in the world,
But often it's the obvious we miss:
A billboard, a street sign.
                                                    On that college tour,
The basement entrance warned me, "Mind Your Head!"
Years later, the hiking trail said, "Watch Your Step!"
The demolition placard said, "Stand Clear!"
And now a city crosswalk sign reminds me
To "Walk With Light!"

April 28

In the corrugated heat
Above an asphalt roof,
A carpenter bee, riding
The rippled light, glides down,
Lifts back to hover a moment,
Veers, and rises again.
With every pass and dip,
Its shadow comes in focus;
Bee and buzzing shade
Are almost brought together.
Then, up in a thermal rush
Of shingles, it blurs again.

A bee can only touch
Its shadow if it lands
Or dies, both cast as one.
And I, its opposite,
Can only lose my shadow
By jumping, so when I die
I hope that, by a leap
Or somersault of faith,
My heart and darker side
Will focus as a thought
Or perfect prayer that flies
As lightly as the light.

Global Eyes

I taste the lemon in my mayonnaise.
It interrupts my sentence, wanting me
To say, pronounce, a field of rice or maize.
Eyes shut, I see and hear the killer bee
In roadside acres grown in pepper bush.
I see a big Brazilian woman's blender;
She mixes egg and oil into mush,
Then a squeeze of lemon, enough to send her
Into ecstasy. But I'm distraught
About the lemon truck, the diesel fumes,
The ship, the supermarket.
                                        Am I caught
Between my weather and her citrus blooms?
It's a terra incognita.
                                        Reconcile
My winters and her terra cotta tile!

Nominal Problem

A man complained at the Gulf of Mexico
That Exxon-Mobil ruined his horizon
(Not to mention Shell, BP, and Texaco).
His cell phone lost its signal. "Damn Verizon,"
He said and waved its plastic from a dune.
While he lamented melanoma, a bird
Washed up in crude; it looked like a dead cartoon,
Stripped of the line between its life and word.

Oh, weep for the petrol-covered pelican
(The thing! the name!) and rage against the machine,
But Man, whose eye holds more than his belly can,
Adores his diesel and his gasoline.

I lit the bird and headed back to town,
Away from Nature and its burning Noun.

Looking Up through the Cracks

The big picture in the scheme of things
Is not a picture; it's a war of words.
Corner the market and you've coined a phrase.
The bigger piece of the pie defines the terms.

But what about the loser when the trophy
Can't be won? He's always in the gap
Between the catchphrase and catastrophe,
The victor's history and price on the tag.

And while the Right is banning books, the Left
Is banning words.
                                        Stabbed in the back again,
Unnamed, ignoble on the bottom line,
The ones we've called the giver's Indian,
The "spic," the "nigger," they thump the rubber checks
We write for them and pay for *our* mistakes.

Intellectual Lust

It has no pornographic web address;
No spam that tries to sell adultery-dates;
No red-light district where its girls undress;
No late-night cable show that titillates;
No X's side by side like chorus girls;
No all-night truck stop neon signs.

This is another kind of lust that swirls
Around the pantheon of learned minds,
Half-naked sirens for the curious
That sing the intellect's magnificat
For ships of fools, a song so spurious
It kills the curiosity *and* cat.

But once the scholar ship has run aground
There are no mermaids draped upon the rocks
And no catastrophe of soldiers drowned.
And yet the troubles of Pandora's box
Are everywhere, like prostitutes and pimps,
Enticing you with tongues that move like dancers
Dressed as decorative questions so you glimpse
Beneath their skirts at their exotic answers.

Word-of-Mouth

Amelia Island, Georgia

It hurts my head to see the awkward grace
Of pelicans, the moment when they hit
The rounded water's surface square in the face.
It hurts the pelicans as well, to wit:
They're blinded by the impact over time.
So what's the sense in being so up-ended,
Starving to death and still within their prime,
Unable to see what they once apprehended?
But how they plummet hungrily at fish
Inspires a living metaphor of Mind:
My appetite and will, my frequent wish
To capture Thought and Thing in word, combined
Tongue-in-cheek, in stomach, heart, and soul;
To eat the salty language of it whole.

Rebuilding Babel

The last two women who can speak their tongue,
— Their jungle home became a cattle farm;
Their children say "Baik Baik" in the city's swarm. —
What do they talk about? What goes unsung,
The feeling after sex, the shine of rain?
Names for the plants and animals they ate
Will die with them and birds that find no mate.
Think of the silences they *don't* explain!

Our planet used to be a polyglot,
But, with the death of every dialect,
It reconstructs the mother tongue it spoke
By speaking English. Have we not
Helped leave those women speechless? We erect
A tower that unbuilds what Babel broke?

Reductio ad Absurdam

Thousand Island dressing on Caesar Salad
Evokes two distant and conflicting shores,
A mix of Greece and Rome, both times invalid
As archipelagos and metaphors.

The clever caveman and the scientist
Have shrunk our world until we're at a loss,
And it would take a skilled reductionist
To sort our fitful histories of sauce.

Picture a ship in some Aegean scene;
It sank at port, that storm in AD nine,
Waiting the forty days of quarantine,
Are its amphorae — of oil and wine — still fine,
Or vinegar?
                    Small world! No, Time, and yet
The two together like a vinaigrette.

Credo Quia Absurdum Est

Remember that religion led to science.
Faith was less of a certainty, in fact,
Than curiosity, an old alliance
Between the will and what desire lacked.
Then some in science stood above the mist
Of dead belief to see what eyes could see.
In superstitious faith, the atheist
Divined what it means to be or not to be;
He found no fact inside a miracle,
Like Santa, something to renege.
"Reject the world that's not empirical!
The Easter Bunny lays no chocolate egg!"

Take heart. A credo isn't edible,
But say it, and it tastes incredible.

Eden *Redux* as Apocalypse

An anchor woman said that climate change
Endangers life; the facts of both are linked.
With temperatures above the normal range,
A host of animals could go extinct.
And imagine plants that'll wither in the pith.
But when they're gone, what language will there be
To classify the lack they'll leave us with?
Will anyone unname the busy bee
In nursery rhyme menageries that tame
Both beast and bugaboo? We'll have no use
For Noah's homeward ark and Adam's game
Of lucky dog, prize pig, and mother goose.
And then poor Eve may still not render moot
The Fall with sour grapes of passion fruit.

III.

Double Vision

At Waffle House, they fired her on the spot:
"You talk too much!"
                                        She'd told her customers
That "made" gets "mad" and "poet" goes to "pot"
Without the letter 'e.' The "amateurs,"
She'd said, "inherit everything: the sand,
The stars, the world that only God possesses."

While washing dishes with a bleeding hand,
She'd told them, "through 'possession's' double 'esses'
There's a line that cleaves; things come apart;
'Refrain' means both 'hold back' and 'go again';
Things join in wholes of which they are a part."

She "touched" the people. Was it such a sin?
Her broken pencil left a double line
On my tab, both legible as one design.

Apocalyptic Almanac

"The Earth exists embedded in itself,"
Said Heidegger. I don't know what he meant.
Chateaubriand said, "Trees precede what men
Call 'civilized,' and deserts follow."
Hell,
I've sawn the firewood from the graveyard trees.
I still have keys to houses that have burned.
Is there a nameless evil I've incurred,
Or have I spread it? Was it born with me?

I dreamed that Helen Keller taught me how
To pour the world across my hands, to read
The planet's head, its own phrenology.
I saw its artful circles plotted out
In GM crops, its autobahns designed
In cloverleaves of Portland, sand, and lime.

Fallen Fruit

The very day that Ingmar Bergman died,
I read a book on pictures, words, and sums
That glossed the first time Helen Keller cried.
Beside me, there were piles of rotting plums,
The neighbor's summer windfall gone to waste.
A yellow jacket landed on my chair,
And colors on its abdomen were spaced
So perfectly I couldn't help but stare.

My daughter asked me, "How are shadows made?"
And, blinded by how clear and luminous
Her eyes were then, I suddenly felt afraid
That I would disappoint the obvious,
The sensual world in words I'd merely choose.
But then my son asked, "What if time could slip?"
His Time! Her Light!
                                        Though Eden's ingénues,
Their minds and garden-hearts could already lisp
In metaphors that I would not dispute,
Could see the world that isn't there, could smell
The sweetly fecal scent of fallen fruit
That issues out of symbols like a spell.

I can't protect them; they were bound to see.
The Fall was knowing what it meant "to stand"
Then painting the paradise that used to be
In language that could raise it from the sand.
Thinking in pictures, feeling in words, I cried

When Bergman died, like Helen when she knew
The beauty of the world, what liquefied
Across her hands that felt and wrote and drew.

Littoral Translation

Morning unrolled the day's velocity
Across a shed roof where, all night, the frost
Had left a texture perfectly embossed.
Each melting letter of its tapestry
Lit up and died along the shadow's zone;
In such minute degrees, the moving swath
Illuminated what became a cloth
Where every present stitch in time was sewn.

By such degrees, all boundaries are blurred.
And, fact or fiction, don't we also "shine"
At certain times: the hurricane, the quake?
Then, like the lovers in Pompey who stirred,
Though barely, stories deep in ash so fine,
We'll dream of words and things, and never wake.

Imago Reperta

Who isn't fascinated by Lascaux,
The earliest of French impressionism,
Sophisticated renderings that glow
And gallop in our lamps' anachronism?
Its zodiacs of animals still dance
As symbols of things we dimly recollect:
The horse, the hunt, the after-dinner trance.

Did they envision *us*? Do we suspect,
In the long thaw, that undiscovered caves
Contain more murals underground, telling
The same *histoire* along forgotten naves?

I close my eyes, and even more compelling
Are passages of thought I've yet to find
As painted dreams and prayers inside my mind.

Dream Vocation

It happened in a country like Tibet,
My dream: I'd climbed a mountain pass and found
Where locals wrote their slips of prayer and let
Them rot between the rocks and on the ground.
Asleep, not feeling any reverence,
I picked one out and saw to my surprise
That it had been addressed to *me.* Its sense
Was mystical; it said, "With open eyes,
You'll never see the proof that God exists,
Only the evidence: the world, the ice,
The snowballs melting in your open fists."
Shutting my eyes in dream, I woke up twice
And groped around for the prayer but couldn't find it,
Nor could I remember who had signed it.

The Culture Counter of the Counter Culture

The Berkeley drug store called "Ganesha's Trunk"
Sells everything you need to be enlightened:
A book on all things Christian to de-bunk;
Many more on how to make awareness heightened;
A personal Om machine with soothing sounds;
A bamboo fountain "for serenity";
Hemp filters for organic coffee grounds;
Hemp clothes; Tai Chi on CD-rom; Chai Tea;
A shaman "box-gift-set"; brass Tinghas Bells;
The Dali Lama action figurine;
A candle Venus of Villendorf that smells;
The *Llama Dolly* children's magazine.
It's all for sale, up at the culture counter,
High-priced for children of the counter culture.

Guru

The heavy-footed man in tennis shoes
Wears baggy pants and cultivates an air
Of inner peace he had the sense to choose.
He wears his soul with new-age debonair,
What his admirers try their best to follow,
All the transcendent smiles and kindly deeds,
The bumper-sticker truth they gladly swallow.
Life's an open door of hanging beads.

OMG

It's been included in the OED
As acronym!
                    Is this a sign of the end
That our most common sacrilege would be
Approved (unspoken though) for us to "send"?

It's bad enough to *say* the name in vain.
Mon Dieu! Good Lord! So having it sliced and diced
As silent letters might be *more* profane.

But someone mutters "Jesus Fucking Christ!"
And it stabs my inner Pharisee to death.
The Hebrews wrote only consonants, the G
Of God without the holy vowels, the breath
Abbreviated.
                    As a curse or JFC,
It's still a prayer on every thumb and tongue,
And heaven hears it like a bell that's rung.

Irreconcilable

It kills me that the faith of Abraham
And Isaac, Ruth and Mary, John and Paul
(What put the poetry in David's every psalm,
And opened up the covenant to all,
And taught Augustine how to love again,
And let St. Francis speak in tongues to birds,
Erected Chartres and Notre Dame in stone
And made a Bach cantata speak like words)
Is also what inspired the holy wars
And justified the trade of certain races,
The desecration of our natural spaces,
The burning of witches, heretics, and whores,
And gets misconstrued by men in pointed hoods
Or in camouflaged militias in the woods.

Modern Church Architecture

Vinyl siding and a slight steeple.
Mega barns for boring white people.

Chapel of the Cross

Chapel Hill, North Carolina

It's no coincidence that, on the ceiling,
Lathing and beams above where people sing
Give both a formal air and barn-like feeling,
Evoking the nascence of our shepherd-king.

Chapels were often built like barns, their wood
Well-hewn or not at all, logs hoisted there
As perfect joist or branching rafter, what could
Suggest a post-and-lintel cross, or the air
Whistling under forest canopies.

By vaulting the *firma* to the firmament,
Some churches still preserve a sense of trees,
A structured grace, both lithe and permanent,
Building us up if we've obeyed or sinned,
Breathing the architectures of the wind.

Bruegel's Harvesters

The tree is central, though slightly to the right,
And partially conceals the village kirk
In foliage and limbs. Today, we might

Assume that nothing meaningful could lurk
Along that line where earth and heaven meet.
We drift below where men are hard at work,

Scything the summer into sheaves of wheat.
That's what we do, believing less and less
In anything from "demon" to "paraclete."

And even Bruegel was a great success
By painting the peasants for the peasants' sake,
Not glossing principles that Popes profess.

But look how the steeple and horizon make
The crosshairs of a transit lens, a joint
Of intersecting planes. Was that a mistake?

Does being hopelessly down-to-earth anoint
Amnesia or a willful ignorance
Of any elevated vantage point?

The only way that Bruegel could have once
Conceived of all this panoramic scene
Was by a similar reconnaissance;

He must have been in a tree himself and seen
The diving vista with a bird's eye view,
Leveling skyline and windows in between.

If anything, those windows hold a clue.
Imagine you could zoom in close enough
To see what isn't bidding God adieu.

You'd see reflection call the painter's bluff.
You'd see perspective vanish back across
The field and through the leaves that luff

Above the women who, without a boss
In sight, have stopped to catch a little rest.
That man who seems completely at a loss,

Asleep beside them, his head and shoulder pressed
Against the tree, what is that by his head?
Is it a pillow, or a palimpsest

Where Bruegel drew and then redrew the head
A little lower? It's like a shadow, or a ghost
Of where he was, and both of them look dead.

The old head faces up and back to the coast,
That world, governed as it was and named
By what the Church said happened to the host.

The other's eyes are shut, but his face is aimed
Exactly at the place where, like a stare,
He looks at Bruegel, where the scene was framed.

His line of sight and Bruegel's eyes would share
The focal point projected from that spire.
It begs the question: Was Bruegel really there?

Or is he *in* that steeple, eyes on fire,
Gazing away from everything he knew
To something promising and also dire?

What *is* the painting then? If this is true,
Then Bruegel and that sleeping harvester
Are looking from these oils right at you!

We are the painting! a vision, as it were,
Subjunctive mood turned inside out to show
The painter more than waking dreams infer.

For good or ill, we shape our own tableau,
An industry of steeples made from hay.
We reap the world and whirlwind as we go.

We draw our own conclusions every day.
Our only faith is the measurement of Time.
Our towers never call us back to pray.

The belfry *cloche* that churches used to chime
Became the clock that told the marketplace
What makes a figure whole and what is prime.

But when we've traded everything but Grace,
When artistries of Man have run their course,
The only God will be the human face

That's unafraid of horsemen or the horse,
Unless we turn and look at Bruegel there
Behind the glass of our forgotten source

Where something spirals up and down the stair
Between a matin and a vesper, free
And timeless, singing a hymn, a living prayer
That's still defining everything we see.

Nude Descending an Escalator

She doesn't have to move,
And being still, her shape displays
A sinking feeling that can prove
A point beyond her flaccid gaze,
That being carried motionless
Is rarely ever beautiful,
Like watching someone's passionless
Concern for being dutiful.

And in this solid stance
Of glib, involuntary whim,
Her modern ease allows no dance,
No simple timpani of limb.
Her beauty used to come in stride
But now, if she stepped down and swayed,
Her body might become the ride,
A moving stair, machined and staid.

Nashville Wasteland

"The lamp of the body is the eye;
If therefore your eye is clear,
Your whole body will be full of light."
— *Matthew* 6:22

I.

Topography and steering linkages
Define the morning: brake, gear down, and turn
With country roads that follow on the heels
Of early settlers and buffalo.
Terrain determines where the curves will be,
So even faster than the speed of feet
Or hooves, as I have gone today by truck,
I couldn't help but notice how a region
Draws a traveler along like water,
Or like paintings that direct the eye
To move within a frame that doesn't move.

A landscape painting is a kind of writing.
How you see determines what you read.
And backroads have that kind of penmanship
As in the painted languages of art.
It's written in a grammar of the ground.
The way you ride determines what you see.
So through the cursive eloquence of fields
I've read the drybrush lines in hills and fences.
It's a language where the stationary
World is spoken on by how we move.
The slower you go the faster you read.
The more you read the slower you want to go.

My scenery and speed make sense until
I hit the four-lane widening construction.
Dozers level hills and fill the valleys,
Straightening their imminent domain,
And leaving ox-bow curves of country road
Abandoned by the stream's meandered path.
Topography becomes irrelevant.
My cursive drawing turns to cursory,
As if the language of an interstate
Is written in a foreign dialect,
Oblivious to local idiom.
It never stops for breath or punctuation.
Roads deliver you from here to there,
But interstates are meant to take you FAST.
The countryside is immaterial
And instantly I notice hell-bent faces
In the cars and trucks that rifle past me:
No small towns with all their school bus zones
And yokels who don't signal when they turn.
I can't keep up. My engine throws a rod
And I'm dead still beside the after-gust
Effrontery of tractor-trailer wind.
If I had broken down at lesser speed
I might have been a little less annoyed.
I could have used a farmer's phone for help,
But here there are no farmers near the road
Where higher expectation generates
Enormous disappointment, even rage.
I kick the bumper. I'm bent out of shape.

Epiphanies occur this way, they say,
Beside the beaten path when vantage point

Has been redrawn by someone else's hand
So everything is altered, new and strange.
My flash of insight happens on the shoulder
Watching faces in the passing cars,
Because I realize that in my rage
I've only acted out, in pantomime,
The vulgar language of the interstate
That barks and rattles like an auctioneer
Against the lay of the land, instead of with it.
If an interstate were like a painting
It would be the kind of modern art
That always Frankensteins the human form,
The kind that's always playing hard and fast
With all the rules of nature and technique.
Dissatisfaction with the here and now
Creates a haste that can't be satisfied.
Impatience is the purest form of rage.
It mutilates the land it passes through
And likenesses of bodies on a page.
Its speed disfigures everyone it claims.
I know because my anger on the road
Has rendered me, as if in my own bile,
Like figures by the painter, Francis Bacon:
Popes and lion tamers, friends and foes,
Too overcome with being comfortable,
Well-fed, and safe to take it any more.

II.

Into the sprawl of Nashville-onto-Nashville,
Down the miracle miles of gasoline,
Adult book stores, and fast food jungle gyms,

And past the knick-knack malls of hokey shops
Where big-haired women buy their potpourri,
My truck is towed to "U.S.A.-Kar-Nation"
Where mechanics sport their pin-up girls
In topless poses over calendars.
One customer who looked too long and hard
At one of them provoked the tire man
To point and chortle, "She's an eye-full ain't she?"
I'm uncomfortable. I also looked,
Like in the checkout lines of grocery stores
Where fashion magazines for women tout
"The Latest Method to Unleash Your Lust;"
"Superior Sex in Seven Easy Steps;"
And on the cover there's a woman who,
Half-dressed for success and looking smug as hell,
Will gladly testify to claims inside.
I tend to look away, but here in what
I've already named, "The Carnal Garage," I've seen
The spitting image of a grease-monkey's dream.
No one could argue with her being there,
God love her, she's so obvious to all.
I try to think what Jesus would have done
If Mary Magdalene were here today.
She might be like Miss April on the wall.
I looked, so who am I to throw a stone.

The head mechanic tells me I should wait
Until the special part comes in for him.
I wait. A yuppie student next to me
Is telling someone jokes about the man
Who lost his penis in an argument.
You've heard the ones I mean: He lost his head;

She really got the upper hand on him;
No pen-is mightier than the sword.
That doesn't strike my funny bone the way
It does the others here, remembering
A man who'll get no rise from anyone.

The television in the waiting room
Has preached an hour's infomercial on
The virtues of an exercise machine
That promises a chubby mother-of-three
The kind of abs she had before the kids.
Her preacher looks at her with hungry eyes.
I know he's seeing through her leotards —
There's something in his gaze, the pupils hung
So heavily below the upper lids,
I know that something's altered in his soul,
A slight malaise he nurses for effect.
I study the eyes a minute.
                                        I'm compelled
By something, not his message, more the sense
That it's the part of déjà-vu you get
Before it freaks you out by coming back.

III.

Outside, the Nashville sprawl is widening.
Its metal roofing and the printed awnings
Sell new things amid the glassy miles
Of PoMo Architecture's single story.
Park bench ads and billboards, painted busses,
All the signs and wonders of the city
Meant to sell a hunger more than things,

They hock a sickening pastiche of needs
With iconographies of want and envy
So that every bodily urge has come
To represent itself in pictograms
And logos, cartoon versions of motif.

Even images of art become
A fleeting food for thought by signifying
Objects of desire that don't require
The interaction of museum goers:
Vermeer is advertising vinyl siding;
DaVinci sells shiatsu body sessions.
It's the slick, commercial dialect
Of eight-lane thoroughfares and overpasses
Boiled down to its mentality.
The speed of cars became the speed of seeing.
All commuters need to do is flick
Their vision on and off all day the way
A television screen goes on and off
So fast you think it's always blue.
They needn't look between the images
To find a meaning other than the flash.
But after years of "blinks" that consummate
By speeding up the eye, projector-style,
The mind that hides behind a darting glance
Can't see a thing that's not subliminal.

Vague is the pain it causes in their brains.
They're all bent out of shape and don't know why.
Such *ennui* is real enough to touch,
And *angst* is palpable in every face.
The cities offer remedies galore

From plastic surgery to fortunetellers.
And it's visible across the street,
An herb boutique-slash-family tanning booth
Where anyone can darken panty lines
And bring the kids along as well to keep
Their faces looking summery all year.

Next door there is the Total Fitness Center,
Built, it seems, entirely of glass
So people on the street can see inside,
Which is entirely the point. The view
Is pretty good if what you want to see
Is women doing battle with their bodies,
Winning here and there, a war they'll lose
Against unsightliness and cellulite.
No doubt they've also gone for breast implants,
A lipo-suck, a little nip and tuck
To hide the signs of age and help them build
Impressive boobs, the perfect piece of ass,
Effects of flesh they know will drop men dead.

And that's the other reason why they come.
You know it by the way they arch their backs
On stationary skis and bicycles:
To draw an eye or two from sweaty men
Who put their shoulders to the wheels
Of work they try to make look effortless.
Above a door it says, "No Pain-No Gain."
And so they grimace into shows of strength,
And do it well, their buttocks looking like
Kielbasa tucked in casings that will break,
Their necks and arms so muscle-bound that when

They strain to raise a bar with confidence
Their bodies illustrate the way it feels
To see a man become a piece of sausage,
A mental embolism that expands,
Prolapsing into hemorrhoids of thought.

IV.

I need fresh air and walk behind the shop.
But even there it's more of the same, except
For being still and relatively silent
Like a cemetery. This is a junkyard,
Rusted clunkers that were dumped in rows.
Ironically they're even facing east
As if awaiting rapture. But mechanics
Only cannibalize their body parts
For other cars. Not one will do for mine.
There's every make and model represented,
From convertibles to passenger cars
To pick-up trucks that smell of tackle boxes
Full of ancient, melted fishing lures.
Their twisted carcasses are full of junk
Like empty beer cans and the shattered glass
From last hurrahs that came and went with a bang.
For sport I write in pencil on a hood,
"Wild to be wreckage forever," and that seems right
Since for a little while I feel a thrill
To be surrounded by the carnage here.
Mortality can lend a peacefulness,
As in Montaigne's essay where he says
That being alive is learning how to die.
But these memento moris are machines —
Alas, poor Taurus, Nova, Aerostar!

Just then I look inside a Cressida
And through its window staring up I see
The opened pages of a centerfold.
A woman spreads her thighs and opens out
Her vulva by its eyelids to unveil
A pupil so intractable and blind,
You know she only learns to see the world
By being seen herself. Her name is Candy.
She's from Boca Raton, and "loves to fuck."
I want to ask her why it's come to this,
But she's too busy whispering that she
Would have me Now, right here in effigy.
So all I'm feeling is the planet spinning
Faster and faster, so she'll get her wish
To skip preliminary ceremonies
Like a date or weddings, even foreplay,
Whispering, "avoid the rush, come early."
I try to say, "I'd rather come on time,"
But she's not listening.
                                        I look away,
Annoyed. Have I reacted on her terms?
I try imagining her father's face,
Or what was left of it when alcohol
Or speed or rage consumed him like tornadoes
That seek out the nearest trailer park.
But all I see is Bacon's portrait of
The screaming pope with hanging sides of beef.
And through the lids of Candy's vertical smile,
I see that infomercial preacher's eye
Inside the face that Bacon left a blur.
It's then my *déjà -vu* comes back around
Because I'm standing in his abattoir-

Cum-sanctuary where he reigns in filth,
Presiding in detritus of the eye.
Then what comes out of me is like a moan
In decibels so low I can't be heard.
I'm like the nurse in *Battleship Potempkin,*
Crying out the quintessential wail
Of human woe. But that's a silent film.
Nobody hears a thing from either of us.
I feel like vomiting, but holding my head,
I run back into the carnal garage and wait.

V.
The customers have changed. It's getting late.
They've turned the television off for now.
I hear the static of florescent lights
And air compressor wrenches in the shop.
Beside me there's an old man with a paper
And his hands are trembling so much
The pages shuffle softly through his fingers.
It's the sound of sand in an hourglass
If you should hold one up and hear the day
Collapsing grain by grain in the nicks of time.

The world is always trying to get ahead
By taking shape from something else.
It's always in a hurry, beating the clock,
Or melting it, as in a Dali painting.
Does either way deform reality?
Time is only how the eye relates
To light and its incessant, blinding speed.
It's light that causes time to pass so slowly

In relation to the turning earth.
Impatience always leads to ugliness
But light makes anything look beautiful.

It doesn't have to change velocity,
Like now, the sun approaching crepuscule
Around where metal buildings spread themselves
On lots too big for what they hope to be,
I can't help noticing how perfectly
The light has turned in evening dishabille.
It washes down the strip-mall ugliness,
Undressing it, exposing what's beneath,
And gives the world a loveliness it lacked.

At six o'clock the day's recumbent glow
Floods in our waiting room and covers us.
A pregnant woman sits across from me
And she's so radiant it almost seems
As if she caused the sudden flush of light,
And then I *know* she did and want to press
My ear against her belly so to hear
The rapid ticking of the heart in there.

Oh, Jesus, isn't that the fullness of time
And why it took a woman giving shape
To more than I will ever comprehend
For you to make your body true to its word?
Soon I'll be a traveler again,
Returning home where my own wife is waiting
Also great with child and radiant.
I'd ride a horse or donkey or even walk,
Except that I'd be killed across the hood

Of some spread-eagle, Chevrolet Camaro
Driven by a man who wears no shirt.
But even though I'll take the slower roads
And take my time, I'll get there soon enough,
Like heavenly bodies moving in due season,
Always coming around and right on time.
My eyes are clear. My body is full of light.

Hope

"So we fix our eyes not on what is seen, but on what is unseen. For what is seen is temporary, but what is unseen is eternal."
— *II Cor.* 4:18

This mystery may seem a flimsy thing,
Unable to support itself, much less
The weight of all your deepest pondering.
Think of the mind, however, and confess
That what informs the brain remains content
To hide its spine and keep its name discrete,
Like iron bars embedded in cement:
The "mystery" of re-enforced concrete.

Spiro / Spirare

A plastic bag and shadows from it range
Across a wall and tree; what isn't there
Impels them, making them shift and rearrange
In shapes that vanish *and* appear in air.
Each eddy makes a Fibonacci shell;
No, actually, it imitates the form
That might inhabit one in a tidal swell
Of calcium.
                    The spiral of a storm
That spawns in Asian waters also curls
An inland lake; and funnel clouds that plague
The prairie lands; and what in little girls
Will crash as waves that are anything but vague.
So even the bag that fills, unfills — descend,
Ascend — inspires me; no, not bag: The Wind!

Snowman Argument

The snowman looks a little worse for wear,
Melting away from his intended ties,
However slim, to Man, to me; his hair
Made from a broken mop, his acorn eyes,
They cease to imitate their maker's face.
"Props in a childhood theater of lies,"
The poet said. It's true, we limn our race
In clay, paint, stone, and word, though each, like ice,
Forgets the living likenesses we trace,
As if the arts were nothing but a vice
Of verisimilitude, analogies
That don't ring true then fade to fail us twice.

But if our metaphors and similes
Are only simulacra we assign,
Does nature have its similarities
Apart from how we draw a common line?
If we were gone, would all our mirrors melt
To nothing like the snowman's vain design?
Dust in the window light where I had knelt
Appeared to ricochet at random, drifting,
Darting, lacking a pattern spun or spelt
From entropy except for how the sifting
Particles resembled swarms of gnats
Or microscopic life that's always shifting.

We don't need scientists who read the stats
And call the motion "Brownian" to see

That correspondences exist in cats
And rats despite the animosity
They show each other. I watch the snowman fade
To nothing, but what approximated me
Is similar to how my mind was made,
Imagined in an image I can know
Each time I see the "somethings" that have stayed
With parallels in sand or wood or snow.
I am most like a snowman in the sun,
And most alive, when, also melted low,
I sense affinity and joy, made one,
With whom I suffer in comparison.

Satanic Christmas

The Devil with his flask of Himbeergeist
And mammon cakes appraises England where
His minions sing "A London Derrière"
And beat the dickens out of Christmas lights.

The painful thought of that Nativity
Provokes him less when no one knows how "Bedlam"
Came from mispronouncing Bethlehem,
How X-mas came to lack naiveté.

But even though the holiday is lost,
It irks him when the traffic lights that flash
Red, green, and gold approximate the past
In festiveness that always leaves him cross.

He doubts his cause. No, bored, he spends the day
Possessing Mrs. Clause and snowman shapes.

Out on My Word

No sooner was I born and on my feet,
Than I'd been seized, arraigned, and thrown in prison.

They said that, in addition to my flaws,
My birth had been a capital offense.
The judge's verdict: Life!
                                        I'm a dead man walking.

Time is the cradle and the jail of fate
Where light falls sawn through colored bars of a prism.

But keeping the witness stand I took, talking
In death-row dialects, I'm now convinced
My sentence has an independent clause.

Until there's nothing left of my grammar but dust,
I'm free to testify, in rigmarole
Or song, about the sad *and* glamorous
Appeal of being condemned and out on parole.

Seriously Funny

For Alan and Callie

Have you heard the one about the boy
Who tried to eat the funny papers?
In nineteen thirty-five, the things
Were printed in a toxic ink;
He swallowed Li'l Abner and died!

No joke! But the funny thing is how
We hop along from frame to frame,
Slap happy, loco, eating it up,
And rarely realize that life
Is a comic strip, a play on words,
A bawdy tale of potty talk,
Then bedroom humor, and back to the potty.
Innuendo and out the other!

And a joke is just a little plot,
A short beginning, middle, end,
A tiny eschatology
That's often scatological.
What do these folks have in common:
Willa Catheter, Urethra
Franklin, Enema Lazarus,
Lafcadio Hernia? Don't laugh!
Or go ahead and bust a gut,
Or, better, laugh to keep from crying.
We all end up like them, and then
We all become that boy, a dead
Cartoon with X'es on our eyes,
The joke on us. Get it? Get it?

And *commedia* and "comedy"
Are not the same, from *Komoidia:*
"A party song for poking fun."
And "fun" is a tricky word to bandy.
It used to be more practical: a hoax;
A way to cheat or double cross;
The funny money of the heart.
But it buys a little time, or dulls
The memory of Now enough
To let us taste eternity,
Each joke a small here-after, a heaven
Where everyone is innocent.
Guffaws avoid our fatal flaws.

So tell another. At the punch line,
Feel the nirvana of no *mañana.*
The moment. The middle.
The life ever laughter.

Telos

"Future Readings" for a quarter; the cards;
The tea leaves; Talmud numbers; Mayan clocks
That tell us Time will end in twenty-twelve;
The Book of Revelation;
Save your breath.
I've got the skinny on the low-down: Death!
We're gonna die, which isn't knocking the bards
Or carvings on apocalyptic rocks.

Man, even pills expire.
So why not shelve
The matter of impending human doom.

Under hips and valleys of your body's room,
The post-and-lintel of your shoulder bones
Supports the walls that girdle your peaceful zones.

Let breathing be a comfort to you there.
Delight in the softness of your eyebrow hair.

Ruach

When I die and breathe my last,
It won't be in or out.
I'll *take* my final breath,
Haling the silence of glass,
Glass that isn't a solid,
But slowly cooling back
From molten silica,
The unheld breath of time.

Once dead, I'll see the moon
As close as my hand, like this.
Who cares if there's any water
Trapped inside its rocks
Like all the water trapped
In Bible stories, water
God brooded over, parted,
Walked on, turned to wine?

I'll see the story of time
Made clearly visible;
I'll see my final breath
Annealing, a miracle
Of clarity, of silence
Of water's opposite,
A perfect silence drawn
From my blood, my noise.
Amen.

Questions in a Doctor's Waiting Room

For Nathan Oliver

I.

I want to fall asleep, and enter the slipstream,
Liminal land of threshold, edge, and stile.
Call it a sliding scale. I'll pay when I please.

But sleep is difficult when all the walls
Are covered with cheesy art:
Watercolors from a photograph,
Life-size poster-prints of watercolors.
On the floor: linoleum made
To look like tile, imitation tile.
Life imitates. . .oh, what do you call it? Kitsch?
So there, I've given it a name. Now sleep!
I would, but how? Everywhere the world
Is full of hybrid creatures needing names,
A post-Edenic problem.
                                        After the fall
Who's up to such an Adamantine task?
I'm trying not to think of all the junk
Somewhere awaiting nomenclature, tagged
And catalogued against ignominy.

Are they asleep, like seeds that need a drop
Of something slippery to call them forth?
It's slippery business, melting the oleo
Of bastard substance, rendering the essence

By palaver made innocuous
To hide the partly real, partly fake.

All margarine is imitation butter,
Barely not linoleum.
I say,
"Linoleo," the nectar of the Nauga.
That's the animal they raise in Texas
Grazing it on fields of astro-turf
To make non-dairy creamer and topping whip.
Its fur is polyester, virgin acrylic.
Its skin becomes the finest naugahide.

Have I gone mad? Am I too sick for words?

II.
There's an elderly woman next to me
Talking about her ugly scarf.
She saved
The cotton from expensive medicine bottles,
Spun it into yarn she could knit,
And wrapped it around her neck.
She's telling me
She has a thyroid problem and the scarf
Is called her, "Dollar Collar."
I'm awake!
She says it again, "This is my Dollar Collar."

I can tell it helps her, not the scarf,
But having made an arbitrary thing
Of worthless value just to give it a name,

A separate peace for things that do not mean.
She calls them to their senses.
                                                  She'll be well,
I know it, though for me it's not as certain.

A nurse is at the door. She's called my name.
I must stand and answer to be healed.

The Author

WIL MILLS, the son of agricultural missionaries, grew up in Brazil and Louisiana. After earning his BA and MA in theology from the University of the South, he worked at a variety of jobs, including carpenter, sawmill operator, and baker. He also served as the Kenan Visiting Writer at the University of North Carolina at Chapel Hill, and as the Writer-in-Residence at Covenant College in Chattanooga. His poetry was published in *Poetry*, *The New Republic*, *The Hudson Review*, *The New Criterion*, and many other journals. His debut collection, *Light for the Orphans*, was published in 2002, and his *Selected Poems* in 2013. Until his death in 2011, he lived in Tennessee with his wife Kathryn and their two children, Benjamin and Phoebe-Agnès, first in a house that he built himself in Sewanee, then, later, in Chattanooga.

www.ingramcontent.com/pod-product-compliance
Lightning Source LLC
Chambersburg PA
CBHW020612310726
48979CB00008B/1444/J
9781939574220